Copyright © 2024 by Shevon Griffith

All rights reserved.

This book or any portion thereof may not be reproduced or used in any manner whatsoever without the express written permission of the author except for the use of brief quotations in an article or book review.

DEDICATION PAGE

In memory of my mom, Rose Griffith,
who taught me the meaning of strength.

Persistence Log:
How have I been persistent?

I remember. I remember. I remember that very first day.
It was my first day of school, and I didn't know what to say.

I looked around and saw so many new faces.
Many were cuddled in their mommy's warm embraces.

Some looked happy, some looked sad,
some looked scared, and some looked mad!

I remember my tears, and I remember my fears.
I remember thinking,
"Oh no! I'll have to do this for 12 more years!"

I said, "Mommy! Daddy! Please don't make me go!"
They told me, "School is the place where you will learn and grow."

I remember. I remember. I remember feeling weak.
When my teacher asked me a question, I didn't want to speak.

I can't read. I can't write.
I wondered if I'd do anything right.

Ms. Clark's Kindergarten Class

I can't spell. I can't add.
Oh boy, I felt so bad.

I remember thinking, "This is not where I belong."
But then my teacher taught me that persistence makes me strong.

Strength means that I ask for help when I really don't know.
I mean, how else am I going to grow?

Strength means that when I feel hurt or sad,
I use my words. I don't get mad.

I made new friends who reminded me each day
that I can do it! If we work together, we will always find a way.

Can you solve today's riddle?

I'm a color word that is 5 letters long.
My name has the long sound of e.
What color am I?

Does that mean that I will never fall?
No, that is not what it means at all.

It means that if or when I do,
I know that this will always be true:

Things will not always be easy.
Strength is in persistence and persistence is the key.

I will never give up!
I will always believe in me!

www.ingramcontent.com/pod-product-compliance
Lightning Source LLC
Chambersburg PA
CBHW082022050526
44107CB00100B/617